THE LIFE OF
SACAGAWEA

CAITIE MCANENEY

press.

New York

Published in 2017 by The Rosen Publishing Group, Inc.
29 East 21st Street, New York, NY 10010

First Edition

Editor: Sarah Machajewski
Book Design: Katelyn Heinle

Photo Credits: Cover (Sacagawea) Neftali/Shutterstock.com; cover (landscape) Paul E. Martin/ Shutterstock.com; p. 5 (main) VisionsofAmerica/Joe Sohm/Photodisc/Getty Images; p. 5 (inset) Vladimir Wrangel/Shutterstock.com; p. 7 Buyenlarge/Archive Photos/Getty Images; p. 9 Ed Vebell/ Archive Photos/Getty Images; p. 10 https://upload.wikimedia.org/wikipedia/commons/6/66/ William_Clark-Charles_Willson_Peale.jpg; pp. 11, 15 Jean-Erick PASQUIER/Gamma-Rapho/Getty Images; p. 12 https://upload.wikimedia.org/wikipedia/commons/a/a6/Meriweather_Lewis-Charles_Willson_ Peale.jpg; p. 13 https://upload.wikimedia.org/wikipedia/commons/f/fd/Detail_Lewis_%26_Clark_at_ Three_Forks.jpg; pp. 14, 19 MPI/Archive Photos/Getty Images; p. 17 SuperStock/Getty Images; p. 21 Danita Delimont/Gallo Images/Getty Images; p. 23 (main) L.A. Nature Graphics/Shutterstock.com; p. 23 (inset) https://upload.wikimedia.org/wikipedia/en/1/16/Bozeman_Pass.JPG; p. 25 (main) Zack Frank/Shutterstock.com; p. 25 (inset) https://upload.wikimedia.org/wikipedia/commons/b/b9/ Popi_sig550.jpg; p. 26 https://upload.wikimedia.org/wikipedia/commons/0/07/Grace_Raymond_ Hebard.jpg; p. 27 Robb Kendrick/National Geographic/Getty Images; p. 29 Marilyn Angel Wynn/ Nativestock/Getty Images.

Library of Congress Cataloging-in-Publication Data

McAneney, Caitie.
 The life of Sacagawea / Caitie McAneney.
    pages cm. — (Native American biographies)
 Includes index.
 ISBN 978-1-5081-4821-0 (pbk.)
 ISBN 978-1-5081-4784-8 (6 pack)
 ISBN 978-1-5081-4819-7 (library binding)
 1. Sacagawea—Juvenile literature. 2. Shoshoni women—Biography—Juvenile literature. 3. Shoshoni Indians—Biography—Juvenile literature. 4. Lewis and Clark Expedition (1804-1806)—Juvenile literature. I. Title.
 F592.7.S123M38 2016
 978.0049745740092—dc23
 [B]
                                                    2015024420

Manufactured in the United States of America

CPSIA Compliance Information: Batch #BS16PK: For Further Information contact Rosen Publishing, New York, New York at 1-800-237-9932

CONTENTS

WHO WAS SACAGAWEA?

Many know Sacagawea as the Native American guide who helped the Lewis and Clark expedition reach the West Coast. You might even recognize her picture from the one-dollar Sacagawea coin. But who was this amazing Native American woman? Where did she come from, and what **impact** did she have on America?

While it's thought that Sacagawea didn't live past her twenties, she accomplished a lot in her young life. She was a translator for English explorers. She was an explorer herself as the only woman on the first western expedition. And she did all this while carrying her baby son on her back. Sacagawea was **invaluable** to her expedition, and hers is one of the greatest stories to come out of the American frontier.

"Sacagawea," which is pronounced "Sah-KAH-gah-WEE-uh," means "bird woman" in the Hidatsa language.

ONE-DOLLAR
SACAGAWEA COIN

KIDNAPPED AND MARRIED

Not much is known about Sacagawea's early life. Historians believe she may have been born around 1788. She may have been the daughter of a chief. She was born into a Shoshone tribe and lived near the modern-day Idaho-Montana border, in an area known as the Continental Divide. This region runs along the Rocky Mountains.

In 1800, an enemy tribe, the Hidatsa, captured Sacagawea. The Hidatsa war party forced Sacagawea from her home and took her to their village in modern-day North Dakota. She was only about 12.

As a young teenager, Sacagawea was sold as a slave to a French-Canadian fur trader named Toussaint Charbonneau. Despite her age, Charbonneau made Sacagawea his wife, along with another Shoshone woman who had been captured. They lived together in a Hidatsa village called Metaharta.

Life with the Hidatsa was different than life with the Shoshone. The Shoshone moved around a lot, hunting bison, while the Hidatsa grew crops and made permanent villages. They lived in lodges made of soil, such as the one pictured here.

THE CORPS OF DISCOVERY

In 1803, the young United States doubled in size when it acquired 828,000 square miles (2,144,510 sq km) of land from the French through the Louisiana Purchase. The land deal cost America about $15 million—about $293 million in today's money—and included more land than anyone could imagine.

President Thomas Jefferson decided to send an expedition west to explore the new land, chart its features and boundaries, and learn about the native people, animals, and plants there. He hired Meriwether Lewis to lead the expedition, and Lewis asked William Clark to be his partner. Called the **Corps** of Discovery, the crew numbered around 40 people. They were given the best supplies, weapons, and **rations** to observe and chart the new frontier. They navigated the Missouri River in three boats and stopped in a Mandan-Hidatsa village in what is today North Dakota.

THE LOUISIANA PURCHASE

AFTER THE AMERICAN REVOLUTION, THE UNITED STATES WAS READY TO EXPAND ITS BOUNDARIES. A TREATY OUTLINING THE LOUISIANA PURCHASE WAS SIGNED BETWEEN FRANCE AND THE UNITED STATES ON MAY 2, 1803. HOWEVER, THE SET BOUNDARIES WERE UNCLEAR IN THE TREATY. LAND THAT WAS STILL OWNED BY SPAIN AND GREAT BRITAIN WAS IN **DISPUTE**. IN THE 1800S, THE UNITED STATES GOVERNMENT FOCUSED ON STRETCHING THE COUNTRY'S TERRITORY FROM COAST TO COAST, WHETHER IT MEANT FORCING NATIVE AMERICANS OUT, BUYING LAND, OR FIGHTING FOR IT.

The Corps of Discovery traveled the Missouri River on three boats, including a keelboat that was 55 feet (17 m) long. It's pictured in this painting, which also shows Lewis and Clark.

JOINING THE EXPEDITION

Soon, Lewis and Clark met Toussaint Charbonneau, and, later, his wife Sacagawea. This was a stroke of luck for the Corps of Discovery. They would need to buy horses from the Shoshone tribe as they moved west, and Sacagawea spoke Shoshone and Hidatsa. Her husband spoke Hidatsa and French. Therefore, they could become a translating team. Sacagawea could translate the Shoshone language into Hidatsa, and her husband could translate that into French. A member of the Corps of Discovery, François Labiche, spoke French and English, so he could complete the translation. The corps asked Sacagawea and her husband to travel with them.

WILLIAM CLARK

WILLIAM CLARK WAS BORN IN 1770 ON HIS FAMILY'S PLANTATION IN VIRGINIA. AS A YOUNG MAN, HE JOINED A **MILITIA** THAT FOUGHT IN THE NATIVE AMERICAN TERRITORY CONFLICTS ON THE OHIO FRONTIER. HE JOINED THE U.S. ARMY, AND BY 1792, HE WAS A LIEUTENANT. HE WAS THE COMMANDER OF THE CHOSEN RIFLE COMPANY, WHERE HE MET MERIWETHER LEWIS. IN 1803, HIS FRIEND LEWIS INVITED HIM ON HIS EXPEDITION THROUGH THE WESTERN FRONTIER. CLARK'S DETAILED JOURNALS AND MAPS OF THE EXPEDITION ARE AN INVALUABLE RESOURCE.

Sacagawea and her husband agreed to go with them. While they waited for spring, the **pregnant** Sacagawea had her baby.

LEWIS

CLARK

SACAGAWEA AND POMP

On February 11, 1805, Sacagawea gave birth to a boy named Jean Baptiste with Lewis's help. Clark nicknamed the baby "Pomp" for his playful nature.

A VALUABLE ASSET

The Corps of Discovery took up their expedition again in the spring. Sacagawea strapped her baby son to her back and began her journey.

Throughout the journey, Sacagawea was an important **asset** to the Corps of Discovery as a translator. However, her value went far beyond that. As they moved west and encountered Native American tribes, she was the reason the encounters were so peaceful. Many of these tribes would have waged war against the unknown settlers, and the expedition might not have survived. Sacagawea, being a woman, made it clear that the white men weren't soldiers there to conquer their villages, but rather, had come in peace. Sacagawea was able to translate between Indian chiefs and the expedition leaders so they could understand each other.

MERIWETHER LEWIS

MERIWETHER LEWIS

MERIWETHER LEWIS WAS BORN ON HIS FAMILY'S PLANTATION NEAR CHARLOTTESVILLE, VIRGINIA, IN 1774. AS A YOUNG MAN, HE MANAGED HIS FAMILY'S PLANTATION BEFORE JOINING THE U.S. ARMY. BY 1800, HE WAS AN ARMY CAPTAIN, AND THE FOLLOWING YEAR, HE BECAME PRESIDENT THOMAS JEFFERSON'S AIDE-DE-CAMP, OR ASSISTANT. IN 1803, LEWIS WAS MADE COMMANDER OF AN EXPEDITION THROUGH THE NEW AMERICAN TERRITORY. AFTER THE THREE-YEAR EXPEDITION, LEWIS WAS NAMED GOVERNOR OF THE TERRITORY OF UPPER LOUISIANA.

Sacagawea was also valuable because she knew which native plants were good to eat.

SAVING THE EXPEDITION

After leaving the Mandan-Hidatsa village, the Lewis and Clark expedition traveled up the Missouri River. They needed to find the Shoshone tribe so they could acquire horses. Unfortunately, their journey got off to a rough start.

Only one month into their trip, on May 14, 1805, a windstorm nearly **capsized** their boat. The boat held important papers, instruments, and supplies, such as medicine. It also held the records and journals Lewis and Clark were keeping of their observations of the land.

Everything would have been lost if it weren't for Sacagawea. As the others panicked, Sacagawea rescued the valuables, and some say she even dove into the water to grab things that had fallen overboard. Her bravery and calmness during the storm gained her respect among the corps.

Lewis and Clark named a **tributary** of a river that flows into the Missouri River for Sacagawea, who truly saved the day.

SUCCESS WITH THE SHOSHONE

By August, the expedition had reached the Continental Divide. Sacagawea recognized Beaverhead Rock in Montana and knew she was close to the land of her childhood. They knew the Shoshone must be nearby. On August 12, Lewis and a small group crossed the Continental Divide at Lemhi Pass ahead of the bigger party. The rest of the expedition reached them five days later. Sacagawea came face to face with the tribe she had been born into. Imagine her surprise when she discovered her brother was the chief! Sacagawea and Chief Cameahwait were finally **reunited**.

Again, Sacagawea proved to be the most valuable asset to the expedition. Her connection with the Shoshone tribe and her helpful translation of their language helped the expedition get the horses it needed.

This illustration shows Meriwether Lewis meeting the Shoshone tribe.

THE SHOSHONE INDIANS

THE SHOSHONE ARE A PEOPLE WHO ONCE LIVED IN REGIONS OF CALIFORNIA, NEVADA, UTAH, IDAHO, WYOMING, AND MONTANA. THEY WERE SPLIT INTO THREE GROUPS THAT WERE CONNECTED BY A SINGLE LANGUAGE. EXPERTS BELIEVE THAT SACAGAWEA WAS A PART OF THE WIND RIVER OR NORTHERN SHOSHONE GROUP. THE SHOSHONE WERE BISON HUNTERS WHO MOVED AROUND A LOT AND LIVED IN TEPEES, MUCH LIKE THE TRIBES OF THE GREAT PLAINS. TODAY, THERE ARE NINE SHOSHONE TRIBES, EACH WITH ITS OWN RESERVATION.

REACHING THE COLUMBIA

Thanks to Sacagawea, Lewis and Clark's expedition now had the horses they needed. On August 31, 1805, they left the Shoshone to continue their journey. The mountainous landscape proved difficult. Their first challenge was the Bitterroot Mountain Range in the Rocky Mountains. They traveled more than 160 miles (257 km) across the steep Bitterroot Mountains.

On September 23, the expedition reached the other side, which is present-day Idaho. They found a village of the Nez Percé. These friendly Native Americans taught the expedition how to make canoes out of trees. They used these canoes to travel down the Clearwater River near Orofino, Idaho.

By mid-October, they had reached the Columbia River. This was a huge landmark—it was the last waterway to the Pacific Ocean. They traveled down the choppy waters in only canoes.

This illustration shows the Corps of Discovery meeting the Chinook Tribe of the Pacific Northwest on the Columbia River.

THE GREAT PACIFIC

In November 1805, the Corps of Discovery reached the Pacific Ocean. However, winter was upon them. The expedition took a vote on where to build winter lodging. Sacagawea, though only a teenager and a woman, was so respected by this time that she was allowed to make a vote. Her voice, once that of a Hidatsa war prisoner and slave, was now counted as equal to the men of the expedition. They established Fort Clatsop near today's Astoria, Oregon, to wait out the rainy winter.

The expedition was nearly over, but Sacagawea had one last adventure. A whale was stranded on the beach. Clark organized a party to find it for food, and Sacagawea insisted she go with them—finally seeing the Pacific Ocean for herself.

This is Sacagawea and Charbonneau's room at Fort Clatsop.

HEADING HOME

When winter ended, it was finally time for the expedition to head home. Sacagawea's job wasn't over yet, though. As they passed through Shoshone lands, she proved helpful once again. When they reached the area that is today southwestern Montana, Sacagawea helped the expedition find what's today called Bozeman Pass in the Bitterroot Mountains. She remembered it from her childhood and said it was the best way to navigate between the Missouri and the Yellowstone Rivers. It made their return trip much smoother.

For the entire journey, Sacagawea carried her son, Jean Baptiste, with her. Clark named a rock formation near Yellowstone Pompy's Tower after Jean Baptiste, using the nickname he had for the young explorer. In 1806, the expedition returned to the Mandan-Hidatsa village where they first found the young family. Sacagawea's journey was over.

This marker at Bozeman Pass through the Bitterroot Mountains honors Sacagawea.

BOZEMAN PASS

Sacajawea, the Shoshone woman who guided portions of the Lewis and Clark Expedition, led Captain Wm. Clark and his party of ten men over an old buffalo road through this pass on July 15, 1806. They were eastward bound and planned to explore the Yellowstone River to its mouth where they were to rejoin Captain Lewis and party who were returning via the Missouri River.

In the 1860s John M. Bozeman, an adventurous young Georgian, opened a trail from Fort Laramie, Wyoming, to Virginia City, Montana, across the hostile Indian country east of here. He brought his first party through in 1863 and the next year guided a large wagon train of emigrants and gold-seekers over this pass, racing with an outfit in charge of Jim Bridger. Bridger used a pass north of here. These pioneer speed demons made as much as fifteen to twenty miles a day-some days. The outfits reached Virginia City within a few hours of each other.

AT JOURNEY'S END

After the journey, Sacagawea's husband received around $500 and a few hundred acres of land. Lewis and Clark, along with their men, left only a couple of days later. Their journey had been around 8,000 miles (12,875 km) long.

In 1809, Sacagawea and Jean Baptiste followed Charbonneau to St. Louis, Missouri. Sacagawea and Charbonneau had their son baptized, or accepted into the Christian faith through a ceremony. William Clark, having been a dear friend of Sacagawea, offered to take care of Jean Baptiste in St. Louis. He promised to provide the young boy with an education.

In 1812, Sacagawea gave birth to her second child, a daughter named Lisette. That same year, it was reported that Sacagawea had died, probably at Fort Manuel, near today's Mobridge, South Dakota.

Clark took care of both Jean Baptiste and Lisette in honor of Sacagawea, who was only in her twenties when she died.

JEAN BAPTISTE

JEAN BAPTISTE WAS BORN ON FEBRUARY 11, 1805, IN A MANDAN-HIDATSA VILLAGE IN NORTH DAKOTA. THANKS TO WILLIAM CLARK, HE WAS EDUCATED IN ST. LOUIS. HE RETURNED TO LIFE ON THE FRONTIER, WHERE HE MET A GERMAN PRINCE. THE PRINCE TOOK JEAN BAPTISTE TO EUROPE FOR SIX YEARS. JEAN BAPTISTE LATER BECAME A FUR TRADER AND GUIDE, JUST LIKE HIS MOTHER. HE GUIDED A GROUP OF MORMONS TO CALIFORNIA. AFTERWARDS, HE WENT TO LOOK FOR GOLD, BUT DIED IN 1866 BEFORE HE COULD FIND IT.

POMPEYS PILLAR NATIONAL MONUMENT WITH AN INSCRIPTION SIGNATURE OF WILLIAM CLARK

DEAD OR ALIVE?

Although most people believe Sacagawea died in 1812, there are some who believe that she lived to be an old woman. In 1907, Dr. Grace Raymond Hebard, a librarian at the University of Wyoming, stated her theory that Sacagawea actually lived to be 100.

One piece of evidence that Sacagawea may have lived is that her death report only referred to her as Charbonneau's wife. Charbonneau had more than one wife, so it may not have been Sacagawea.

Dr. Hebard released the book *Sacagawea: A Guide and Interpreter of the Lewis and Clark Expedition* in 1932. She wrote of a woman who lived on the Wind River Indian Reservation in Wyoming named "Sacajawea," who was buried on April 9, 1884. The woman's approximate birth year of 1784 is close to Sacagawea's.

DR. GRACE RAYMOND HEBARD

SACAJAWEA
DIED·APRIL 9.1884
A GUIDE WITH THE
LEWIS AND CLARK
EXPEDITION
1805 — 1806
IDENTIFIED 1907 BY
REV. J. ROBERTS
WHO OFFICIATED AT
HER BURIAL

Dr. Hebard's theory may be unlikely, but many people believed Sacagawea returned to her Indian roots after the Lewis and Clark expedition.

SACAGAWEA'S LEGACY

Sacagawea lives on in the American memory even after her death. There are countless monuments and statues dedicated to her around the country. Lemhi Pass became a national historical landmark, and recreation grounds nearby were named the Sacagawea Memorial Area. In Pasco, Washington, there's a state park in her name. Sacagawea Park at Three Forks, Montana, also bears her name. In 2001, President Bill Clinton honored Sacagawea's memory by naming her as an honorary sergeant in the U.S. Army.

Sacagawea is a model of strength and bravery for Americans everywhere. Without her, the Lewis and Clark expedition might not have survived choppy waters, native tribes, and unknown land. She was a loving mother, faithful wife, guide for the U.S. Army, and true adventurer.

Although Sacagawea never had her portrait made, the **depiction** of her face is found on coins, statues, and even stamps.

A TIMELINE OF SACAGAWEA'S LIFE

ca. 1788 Sacagawea is born to a Shoshone tribe in present-day Idaho.

ca. 1800 Sacagawea is captured by the Hidatsa tribe.

NOVEMBER 1804 Sacagawea meets the Lewis and Clark expedition.

FEBRUARY 11, 1805 Sacagawea gives birth to her first child, Jean Baptiste.

APRIL 7, 1805 Sacagawea sets off on the Corps of Discovery expedition.

MAY 1805 Sacagawea saves important items from one of the boats as it nearly capsizes.

AUGUST 8, 1805 Sacagawea recognizes Beaverhead Rock on Shoshone land. She knows the tribe is nearby.

AUGUST 17, 1805 Sacagawea reunites with her brother, Chief Cameahwait.

NOVEMBER 1805 The expedition reaches the Pacific Ocean.

MARCH 23, 1806 Sacagawea and the expedition begin their journey home.

AUGUST 17, 1806 Sacagawea's journey ends when she returns to the Mandan-Hidatsa village in present-day North Dakota.

AUGUST 1812 Sacagawea gives birth to her second child, Lisette.

DECEMBER 20, 1812 One of Charbonneau's wives dies of a fever. She may have been Sacagawea.

1813 William Clark formally adopts Jean Baptiste and Lisette.

1884 A woman dies on the Wind River Reservation. Some believe she was the real Sacagawea.

GLOSSARY

asset: A valuable person or thing.

capsize: To turn over, especially a boat.

corps: A group of people working together on a particular activity or for a particular purpose.

depiction: An image or representation of someone or something.

dispute: An argument.

impact: Strong effect.

invaluable: Extremely valuable or useful.

militia: A group of people who only fight when needed.

pregnant: Carrying an unborn baby in the body.

ration: Food or supplies.

reunite: To come back together.

tributary: A river or stream flowing into a larger river or lake.

INDEX

WEBSITES

Due to the changing nature of Internet links, PowerKids Press has developed an online list of websites related to the subject of this book. This site is updated regularly. Please use this link to access the list: www.powerkidslinks.com/natv/saca